BOARDROOM BALLADS

Bertie Ramsbottom

Bertie Ramifications Ltd

Published by Bertie Ramifications Ltd.
ISBN 0 9508339 0 8

Printed in Great Britain by
Butler & Tanner, Frome, Somerset

Typesetting & makeup by
Midas Publishing Services Ltd., Oxford

For Norman Leyland

Contents

Preface

Apart from rhyming graffiti on the office wall, Business has not proved much of an inspiration to the poets of the English language. Business persons, if I may so describe them, have persistently been the also-rans behind daffodils, larks and lovers in the poetic stakes. Even W.H. Auden and John Betjeman, who gave them brief but scathing notice, moved rapidly on to cripple and tennis-girls!

And so it has been left to Bertie Ramsbottom to correct centuries of neglect and reveal the sensitive souls, the smouldering passions, the hopes, aspirations and anguish thinly disguised behind the pin-stripe and the Boardroom door. From the pages of the *Financial Times* and the *Havard Business Review* he has given voice to the covert cadences of the executive suite and the music of the managers.

Business is not life, but life is quite a business, as Mark Twain would have said had it occurred to him. Bertie Ramsbottom dedicates this book not only to those whose life is business, but to those whose business is life. That way, the publisher says, the sale may be bigger. And that's business...

Ralph Wind
Oxford 198

BOARDROOM BALLADS

THE DECISION MAKERS ⸺

When we come to review
What the managers do
Which explains their superior rating,
We are told it is due,
And their salaries too,
To the size of decisions they're making.

And 'we won't' or 'we will's
A particular skill,
In the managers mainly residing,
Which the rest of the guys
In the management's eyes
Cannot match when it comes to deciding.

Which accounts for the flair,
And the infinite care,
The meticulous search for precision,
Which he daily deploys
In pursuit of the joys
Of the art of the business decision.

But the possible shock
Of his head on the block,
And a nasty response in The City,
May explain why he's prone
Not to go it alone
Till it's nicely diffused in Committee.

So some time may elapse
In the future, perhaps,
Till he rises above his defences;
And, unthreatened by blame,
Can quite openly claim
The applause for its best consequences.

And with so much at stake,
On decisions they make,
It has entered their innocent noddles,
To refer their distresses
To learned professors,
Computers and mystical models.

Now professors express
An intelligent guess
In the language of forecasting science;
And have found divinations,
Expressed as equations,
A hit with their gullible clients.

But decisions, my friend,
And a means not an end
And it's 'how' more than 'what' that may matter;
And the wise are, as ever,
More use than the clever —
Since there's more to decisions than data.

LADY ON THE BOARD ──────

A Board Room is a kind of den
Wholly redolent of men,
Which women mainly get to see
When bringing in the lunch or tea;
But one or two, I would applaud,
Have brought a Lady on the Board,
Either out of great acumen
Or as their "statutory woman".

Either way, the eye detects
Unexpected side effects,
Which tend to make the Board Room rock
To massive metabolic shock,
And leave the gentlemen regretting
A problem of their own begetting.

For here the chauvinistic mind
Seems inescapably inclined
To place, in two main categories,
The ladies central to their worries;
Disparaging, behind their backs,
Their "bomb-shell" or their "battle-axe".

The "bomb-shell" image is a figure
Like Marylin Monroe's, but bigger —
Elegant, but only just,
Clothed about the thighs and bust;
Offering like Eliot's miss
Some promise of pneumatic bliss.

But contrary to male assumption
That pretty blondes have little gumption,
The modern version boasts degrees
Like MBAs and Ph.Ds,
And an intellect as real
As her physical appeal;

A combination which the men
Never hope to see again!
And, envy coupled with desire,
They watch the goddess rising higher
Until, with sunlight in her hair,
She occupies the Chairman's chair.

The "battle-axe" implies a style
More dependent on her guile,
Since her feministic facets
Are seen as insubstantial assets.
Eschewing every pleasure known,
To which the weaker men are prone,
She maddeningly seems to know
Everyone's portfolio;
And, where information's power,
Accumulates it hour by hour,
Until, by process of attrition,
She decimates the opposition

These ancient overtones of sex
Cannot prevent what happens next,
When every Boardroom stands ajar
To women as they really are —
Good and bad, like all the others
Of their gentlemanly brothers;
Revealing — and it really hurts —
The irrelevancy of their skirts!

THE CHAIRMAN OF THE BOARD

Given their elevated stations,
The Chairmen of our Corporations
Cannot be classified at will
By any one specific skill —
Beyond a certain savoir-faire
In politics and staying there.
And Presidents, as sometimes mooted,
Are similarly constituted.

Distinguished generals retiring,
Or Civil Servants due for firing,
Are types for which Directors hanker —
Or, better still, a Merchant Banker.
A decent presence on the telly,
Some readership of Macchiavelli,
Or *titles* — corporations note —
Are things on which investors dote.
And City Editors, despite
Their protestations, love a Knight;
Even the shareholders will shoot
For equities of low repute,
In companies whose only claim's
A Chairman with a fancy name.

But companies which can't aspire
To superannuated Lords — or higher —
Tend to get the top-chair full
On the Peter Principle;
Suggesting that the Founder's son,
While nominally number one,
May be more easy to control
In the Presidential role,
And cause less frequent cataclysms
Than if he actually takes decisions.

I have not been entirely able
To separate the fact from fable;
Or decisively review
What Presidential persons *do*;
Beyond a tendency to shout
If someone tries to get them out —
As evidenced by Fraser's law
That, when Directors are at war,
The incidence of board-room bleeding
Increases with the Chairman's breeding.

Perhaps the most conclusive data
That Presidents and Chairmen matter
Reside in seeing that they all,
Get their portraits on the wall,
A benefaction not decreed
Directors of a lesser breed.
So take a charitable view
Of this elevated few —
At least for this unconscious part
In business sponsorship of art;
And long, then, may we hope to see 'em
Snoozing in the Athenaeum!

PERSONNEL ———————————

Since human beings, I surmise,
Are what companies comprise;
And human beings, what is more,
Are what businesses are *for*;
And since Directors, too, are born
More-or-less in human form;
You might expect the people sector,
To have the dominant Director.

The actuality, I find,
Is mostly of another kind!
And many a well-intentioned fella
Becomes this Board-Room Cinderella,
Who, having learned to buy and sell,
Gets Personnel thrown in as well!
And occupies the twilight zone
Between this function and his own!

Afflicted by his sudden curse,
He looks around for books — or worse,
In his desperate search for rules,
Has recourse to Business Schools;
Discovering that what he thought
He ought to do, he didn't ought,
From strangely incoherent mystics,
Dabbling in Behaviouristics;
Or high on Theory X or Ys,
With hygiene factors in their eyes.

And, mesmerised by hocus-pocus,
He desperately tries to focus
On how it possibly relates
To pickets at the factory gates,
Or maladjusted foremen who
Make wrong advances in the loo;
Concluding that the people part
Is less a science than an art!

There is another school of thought,
To which some companies resort,
In desperation at the war
Between the Board and factory floor.
In this, the said Director gives,
To worker representatives,
Occasional selective looks
At what is written in The Books,
Hoping this may quench the flames
When they next submit their claims.
But, sadly, this enlightened cult,
May have the opposite result,
And give the workers new pretensions
To company cars and richer pensions;
And whet their appetite for passes
To join the upper social classes.

This is really why, I think,
Some Personnel Directors drink,
Preferring to revert to sin
Than face the fact they cannot win —
Before the final revolution
Provides the ultimate solution.

FINANCE

Measured by the linear mile
Of pin-stripe and the absent smile,
Directors of Financial Matters
Lugubriously focus at us
Unenlivened eyes of gloom,
Spreading prophesies of doom.

Armed with thicker files of figures,
His cold and bloodless presence triggers
Terrifying threats of sorrow,
And final bankruptcy tomorrow.
His steely and incisive glance
Demolishes the others' plans,
Reducing to a trail of losses
The forecasts of the other bosses;
And turns their every flow of cash,
Negatively into ash;
Conveying to them all the while,
The notion that they're infantile.
Which, even if it's true,'s a pity
Since connections in the City
Make *his* prospects of survival
Safer at the End's arrival.

The prospect of the finance function,
Administering the Extreme Unction,
Is at one with other signs
That its origin's divine;
Its practitioners convey
That they have not feet of clay;
And their expertise relies
On Mysteries beyond our eyes.

16

They carry their preposterous sham on
As acolytes of God and Mammon;
Invoking on us, if they choose,
The Dreaded Thunderbolt of Zeus
For standing not enough in awe
Of interest rates and Company law;
Or, in our sinfulness, apply
The Sacred Rules of R.O.I.

So this is why directors bow
And scrape before their sacred cow;
Or cannot penetrate the fog
Created by their Board-Room Gog;
And also why ambition withers,
And hope and innovation slithers,
Down the ever-open jaws
Of financial dinosaurs.

I suggest that they be rated
Highest when excommunicated;
And their salaries be docked
Until they get themselves unfrocked.

MARKETING ────────────────

Most boardroom analysts agree
The Marketing Director's fee
Is much more easily earned than others
Among his managerial brothers;
Since, from the moment he can walk,
His quintessential work is talk!
And happily ensconced between
The Sales and the Production team,
Can always blame the one or other
In any little board-room puther.
Sitting on the very fine
Fence between the Staff and Line
He eloquently adumbrates
The failures of his other mates;
And, in the process of the story,
Moves faster on the path to glory.

This, of course, is not to say
That he has no role to play;
And often his superior station
Reflects a higher education,
Which places words at his command,
The others cannot understand;
And so he may prove quite a bargain
In bringing in the kind of jargon
Many business-men may feel
Crucial to their sex-appeal.

Unspeakably deprived is he
Who has no "media strategy";
Or has not bored his loving wife
With theories of "product-life";
And is there hope for such a man
As lacks a decent "payout plan"?

Another Marketing credential
Is inescapably essential,
If he is to show defiance
To criticism of the science;
Never decide on any matter
Without a mile or so of data
Even when it's based on samples
Considerably short of ample.

So Marketing would seem to be
A necessary entrance fee
For Companies whose Boards aspire
To push their business profiles higher
And re-inflate their sagging ids
By making predatory bids
Or other market-oriented fads
Like multi-million dollar ads.

PRODUCTION _____

Production men — it's mainly true —
Lack respect to which they're due;
And spending so much time with spanners
Have slightly questionable manners —
Or so the attitude entails
Of those with cleaner fingernails.
And this is why I think they feel
So relatively down at heel
And carry with them everywhere
A kind of cordon sanitaire,
As if by nature of their fleas
They made their colleagues ill-at-ease.

I must confess I stand aghast
At this sad abuse of caste;
And ask how people who create
Are rated lower in the state,
Than those whose forté, I discern,
Is fiddling a tax return?

One little thing, for what it's worth,
Is, by the nature of his birth,
An engineer will tend to be,
From social classes two or three
And not, like others of his peers,
At Eton in his former years.

And secondly his social graces
Are formed in somewhat different places;
Which makes him, solely in their midst,
Prefer the Black Horse to the Ritz!

But most of all the mystery's
A function of their histories,
And attitudes which favour trade
To what is actually made;
As if to handle a machine
Were, in some curious way, obscene;
But handling stocks and shares, or shipping
Is oh! so marvellously ripping!

Directors of Production, then,
Are really rather special men
Deserving of a better fate
Than they very often rate.

SALES

A long tradition still prevails
By which the Captaincy of Sales
Is offered to the person who
Sold the most in Sixty-Two;
When Joe, with sample bag and brolly,
Took a ticket on the trolley
And, conning many a startled buyer,
Pushed his sales performance higher;
Pulling off as prize again
Two weeks with his wife in Spain.

The route by which he comes to rate a
Board-Room job a few years later,
Is something I do not propose
To track with my enquiring nose —
Even though his colleagues do
Sometimes ask the question too.

The problem which I wish to mention
Concerns the nature of the tension
Which Joe is destined to explore,
Behind the inner sanctum door;
Where idiots who make the stuff,
Cannot offer him enough;
Or, when the market place is sagging,
Ask him why the lads are lagging,
And the transport bays and docks
Are drowning in redundant stocks;
Setting out in pointed phrase
The error of his wasted days.

The product's right and so's the plan!
Get a move on, little man!
Until the final day of dread —
The Chairman's Office letterhead,
Asking him to tea and tiffin,
And bring the latest figures with 'im.
And would he care to bring as well
His Private file from Personnel.

This is how it seems to go
For salesmen of the likes of Joe;
With very little he can see,
By way of counter-strategy,
To out manoeuvre all the others
Behind the safety of their covers.
He'll have to settle for the fate
Of everybody else's hate.

THE CHIEF EXECUTIVE

In among the twisting by-ways,
Convoluted super-highways,
And the leading-to-the-sky ways
    Of the Corporation's Chart;
Where a thousand hopes are tended,
Some fulfilled and many ended,
Dreams and energies expended,
    By the nature of the Art;

At the Apex of the courses,
Where the hierarchic forces
Come together like the Horses
    of the Great Apocolypse;
There, atop the other eyries,
The Chief-Executival Chair is
And, as Primus-inter-Pares,
    The Managing Director sits.

Only He, with touch of feather,
Brings the functions all together,
Nurtures them in every weather,
    Makes the mighty engines tick;
He it is who takes the chances,
Balances the Firm's finances,
Orchestrates the next advances,
    With the carrot and the stick.

He will designate our stations,
Master-mind our operations,
Monitor our allocations,
    Rendering to each his own;
When competitors out-flank us,
Or the A.G.M. cantankers,
He will pacify the Bankers,
    Re-negotiate the loan.

Symbol of our best intentions,
Energiser of inventions,
Soother of our hyper-tensions,
    In the market free-for-all;
When our market share's appalling,
Dividends and profits stalling,
Shareholders for heads are calling —
    His will be the first to fall.

THE NON-EXECUTIVE DIRECTOR

Cogito ergo sum —
   I think, therefore I am —
Is a comforting reflection
   for a passive kind of man;
But more open to discussion
   with the business on the blink
Is the corporate assumption
   that I *am,* therefore, I *think.*

For semantically speaking,
   it's a paradox to give
Definitions of a function
   which is *non*-executive;
Or at least suggests a reason
   for the many people who
Enquire of Non-Executive
   Directors what they *do;*
And many look with envy
   at this curiously thriving
Renaissance of the arcane art
   of non-executiving.

Whatever else it offers,
   this anomalous position
Is rarely calculated
   to give wider range of vision;
Since the typical incumbent
   is exclusively intent
On the Merchant Bank's neurosis
   on the way the money's spent.
Or compliant with the Chairman's
   hesitation to be cluttered
With those who fail to understand
   which side their bread is buttered.
So a rare, protected species
   are the non-execs who tell
Their patrons in the Boardroom to
   politely go to Hell!

The most persistent interests
    reflected on the Board,
Consistently contrasting
    with the ones that are ignored,
Are the lenders and investors who,
    by some strange device,
Are especially enfranchised
    to express their wishes twice;
For having voted on the Board
    to bolster or deplete it,
Can still recall their cash at will
    — both have their cake and eat it.

So composition of the Board
    should really be about
More relevant reflection of
    the views inside and out;
And arguments about the use
    of independent members,
Are insignificant beside
    legitimate contenders
For less-impeded access to
    the corridors of power —
For customers, or women,
    or the workers-by-the-hour.

And in default of all of this,
    the question's rather silly,
Reducing Non-Executives
    to gilding on the lily;
The brighter ones, one hopes, will use
    their privileged position,
To tell the Board a thing or two
    about its composition.

THE BUSINESS CONSULTANT ____

Of all the businesses, by far,
Consultancy's the most bizarre!
For, to the penetrating eye,
There's no apparent reason why,
With no more assets than a pen,
This group of personable men
Can sell to clients more than twice
The same ridiculous advice;
Or find, in such a rich profusion,
Problems to fit their own solution!

The strategy that they pursue —
To give advice instead of do —
Keeps their fingers on the pulses
Without recourse to stomach ulcers;
And brings them monetary gain,
Without a modicum of pain.

The wretched object of their quest,
Reduced to cardiac arrest,
Is left alone to implement
The asinine report they've sent.
Meanwhile the analysts have gone
Back to client number one,
Who desperately needs their aid
To tidy up the mess they made.
And on and on — ad infinitum —
The masochistic clients invite 'em.
Until the Merciful Reliever
Invokes the Company Receiver.

No one really seems to know
The rate at which consultants grow;
By some amoeba-like division?
Or chemo-biologic fission?
They clone themselves without an end
Along their exponential trend.

The paradox is each adviser,
If he makes his client wiser,
Inadvertently destroys
The basis of his future joys.
So does anybody know
Where latter-day consultants go?

THE ADVERTISING AGENCY ___

Let us, if you'd be so kind,
Praise the triumph of the mind
Over more pedantic matter,
Which advertising Agents scatter
Around the edges of the green
Pastures of the Business Scene;
By which, as clients fortunes roll,
Closer to the final hole,
They winkle, from the waiting hearses,
Ever mounting media purses,
For one more advertising burst,
Before the ashes are dispersed.

Words there are not good enough
To match the brilliance of the bluff;
Or adequately to explain
How businessmen of normal brain,
Enter Advertising Houses,
And leave without their shirts and trousers!

The Agency Director who
Persistently performs the coup
Produces, for his rich commissions,
Unique Selling Propositions
Based, as decent Agents should,
On either Sex or Motherhood;
These are, to the Image Makers,
The Freudian Factors which will shake us,
From our apathetic tellies,
To buy some more to fill our bellies;
Or grab, to satiate our greed,
Still more junk we do not need.

Fresh in pinkish shirt and sneakers,
He bounds across the floor to tweak us;
While, busy at his heels, attends a
Retinue of unknown gender,
Heaped with story-boards and charts
And sundry other works of art.

Soon the client's senses tingle
To the orchestrated jingle
Which, the test results declare,
Guarantees his market share;
And, by subliminal recourse,
To some Oedipean force,
Will open, through the hidden eye,
The full capacity to buy.
This time round he cannot fail
To finish with the Holy Grail;
Or see, although the budget's high,
His Sales performance hit the sky.

And on — through dinner at Le Beau;
Perhaps a little girlie show; —
Until our innocent of brain
Is popped discreetly on the train,
Not quite knowing, through the fun,
Who has lost and who has won!

The client's customers may be
A bit less gullible than he;
And more resistant to the guys
Who pulled the wool across his eyes.

IN CORPORE SANO... ────────

The Body Corporate is prone
To some malfunctions of its own,
Too deep for therapy to foil;
And shuffles off this mortal coil,
Leaving the explanatory data
With the Company Liquidator,
And the shareholders in fear
Around the late-lamented's bier.

But, though post-mortems have their use,
There must be methods which conduce
Better to reveal propensities
To death in Corporate Entities;
And, better still, we need prognosis
Of arteriosclerosis,
And other prevalent diseases
Threatening financial seizures.

The more distinguished Company leeches
Start with anatomic features,
Placing, in exact location,
The organs of its operation.
The consequential chart, however,
Tends to beg the question whether
The brain and eyes, as often said.
Are really in the Corporate Head;
Or, by genetical distortion,
Somewhere in the lower portion.

This anatomic imprecision
Suggests the dangers of incision;
For a missed lymphatic cord
Might lobotomise the Board,
Or intended appendectomies
Produce Corporate vasectomies.
So, not-with-standing that it's rife,
Intervention with the knife
At the bottom, may not stop
Hallucinations at the top;
In spite of the seductive pleas
For amputation at the knees
As the favourite reliever
From the Company Receiver.

The Art of Corporate Prosthetics,
Without recourse to anaesthetics,
Bucks the metabolic issue —
The atrophy of Corporation tissue
Through wide-spread paralysis
By elephantiasis;
The most effective cure of all
May be to keep the Body small,
Starting with those wily foxes
— The Corporate Doctors.

THE JAPANESE MENACE ⸻

From London to Bonn and Chicago,
In Zurich, Toronto and Nice;
Every island and archipelago
From Chile, to Holland and Greece;
Wherever Executive People
Slump wearily into their chairs
In the hope that the counting of sheep'll
Do something to lessen their cares;
Wherever the harrassed Director
Turns to sleep for relief when he can;
They awake to the frightening spectre —
Of Inscrutable Men from Japan.

Beleaguered in Basle and Benghazi,
The most robust of Corporate men,
Quake at the vast Kamikaze
Hordes of the murderous yen;
The ubiquitous bland Oriental,
No higher to most than their knee,
Turns giants of industry mental
To an unprecedented degree.
And the threat of the little invaders
Brings a strong, paradoxical urge
For yesterday's eager free-traders
To demand an embargo — or merge.

But it's not just the fact we're losing
The markets that's causing the fuss;
It's these damned funny methods they're using
Which they've clearly not borrowed from us!
Did you ever hear of employers
Giving life-time employment and such?
They're just doing these things to decoy us,
But the Board wouldn't care for it much!

So as for the dubious morals
Or having a National Plan,
With a MITI to sort out the quarrels —
Let's just muddle along as we can!
And a Japanese banker refuses
To behave as he should, we have heard,
By putting the money to uses
Our fellows regard as absurd.

In Bradford, Detroit and Lusaka
There are puzzled executives who
Pray that they'll learn in Osaka,
To do it the way that *we* do.

THE COMPUTER MEN ────────

There was a time we just remember
When, January to December,
We would make, and pack and sell
And pay a dividend as well;
And most directors, good and bad,
Could multiply, subtract and add;
Or run their various Divisions
With time to take a few decisions.

But no one now would dare refute a
Message from his main computer,
Or embark on any caper
Without its thousand yards of paper!
The print-outs and the video-scan
Are quite enough for any man,
So no one really could expect us
To read the stuff *and* be directors.

The Monster answered us with queries,
Gestating through successive series,
And kept us busy days and nights
Like information phagocytes;
Until we thought we'd end the fuss
And make the damned thing work for us!
A process which, alas, consists
Or hiring Systems Analysts.

The Systems Analysts decreed
An urgent, over-riding need
For changing everything we'd got
To ease the information clot —
By relocating functions where
The King Computer would prefer;
Which made the hardware more contented,
But everybody else demented.

So now we have the finest data
Between the North Pole and Equator,
And the poorest market share
Discoverable anywhere!
Systems chiefs outnumber braves,
Crawling through the architraves,
With, to square the whole equation,
Vice-Presidents of Information!

We hoped that they might entertain
Our hyper-active Delphic Brain,
And might graciously afford us
Time for getting in the orders;
But now we're told the thing that's in is
Apples, micro-chips and minis.
No doubt soon we'll change to them —
Plus ça change, c'est plus la meme!

THE BUYERS ──────────────

Up, lads, up: 'tis late for Buying:
Empty pallets never thrive.
Inventories atrophying
Will not keep the firm alive.

Sales are up and stocks are tumbling;
Retail outlets press for more;
And the Works Director, grumbling,
Pounds upon the office door.

Wake: the vaulted warehouse slumbers,
Row on row of empty bays;
Lack of merchandise encumbers
What we need to pay our ways.

Up: the Company's depending,
And the whole production plan,
On the Buying Group's unending
Willingness to play the man.

Move: for Purchasing's a rover,
Must not leave them in the lurch;
Out, beyond the Cliffs of Dover,
Moves the never-ending search.

Up, lads: moping in your beer,
Contravene's the Buyer's creed;
China, Hongkong or Korea,
May supply the goods we need.

Duty calls in two directions;
Buy domestic where you can.
But your colleagues' disaffections,
May suggest a wider scan.

Prices keen and volume ample,
Access simple to the port,
Means that, subject to the sample,
Buyers to the world resort.

Wake: and multiply your contacts;
Probe the corners of the Earth.
And, with favourable contracts
Prove the value of your birth.

Wide the airborne army scatters;
Plastic food on plastic trays;
And, digestive tracts in tatters,
Telex through their flight delays.

Tentative negotiations,
Deep into the night they drag;
Hieroglyphics and quotations —
Till finally, it's in the bag!

See: the loaded trucks, returning,
Make the inventories leap.
Right, lads: now the wheels are turning,
There'll be time enough for sleep.

(with grateful acknowledgements to A.E. Housman.)

THE MULTINATIONAL CORPORATION

When James D. Flaherty O'Rourke
Came from Dublin to New York,
And peddled round his hot potatas,
Few financial commentators
Forecast he was on the brink
Of World Wide Hot Potatas Inc.,
Founding his Global Enterprise
On Chirpy Chips and Handy Fries —
But such are the bizarre gestations
Of Multinational Corporations.

And having made the humble spud
Synonymous with motherhood,
And Chips With Everything the toast
Of every home from coast to coast,
He felt that he should not deny
The culture of the Handy Fry
To less sophisticated clients,
Untutored in potato science;
And ripe, on Wall Street's best assessment,
For World-Wide's overseas investment.

So soon the Hot Potata logo
Flew from Zanzibar to Togo,
With world-wide quality control
By satellite across the Pole;
Linking Chirpy Chip plantations
And process plants in fifty nations,
Including, after tense discussions,
A licence granted to the Russians.

The Tigris, Nile and Orinoco
Were switched from cotton, rice and cocoa
To propagation of the tuber,
As were tobacco farms in Cuba,
On the guaranteed assumption
Of escalating world consumption;
Till all the leading indicators
Were based on futures in potatoes,
With James the undisputed King
Of the carbo-hydrate Ring;
While OPEC in distress reviewed
The synthesis of starch from crude.

Wall Street analysts foretold
A flight from copper, zinc and gold,
And White House strategists demanded
Return to the Potato Standard.
Friedman joined the advocators
Of tight control of seed-potatoes;
And Downing Street was quick to see
Manipulation of P3
As the relevant equation
For final conquest of inflation.

But James was keen to leave decisions
On politics to politicians,
And moved with great reluctance to
Subvert a government or two;
Executives of Hot-Potatas,
Irrespective of their status
And the colour of their skins,
Daily disavow their sins,
Renewing oaths to Handy Fries,
To multinational enterprise,
And James O'Rourke's financial plan
For Global Brotherhood of Man.

41

THE YOUNG EXECUTIVE ⎯⎯⎯⎯

Since I was waist high to a flea,
Papa would take me on his knee
And, from time to time, decree
    The life that I should live;
I'd always thought I'd go to sea,
Or be a farmer such as he,
But he insisted that I be
    A Young Executive.

Acquaintance with my father's boot
Had taught reluctance to dispute
Suggestions he might contribute
    And so I acquiesced;
Requesting what might constitute
The Young Executive's pursuit,
And what it is they execute
    That had so much impressed.

Regretfully, Papa displayed
No detailed knowledge of the trade
Except that it was highly paid;
    And made the resolution
That I could also make the grade
And join the business-man brigade
If I sufficiently displayed
    Some gift for execution.

And so it was I came to buy
A natty suit and hat and tie
And felt that I was quite a guy
    When first I was recruited;
But now, at forty-five, I try
To understand precisely why
And what, before I come to die
    I've really executed.

If Fate would hand me back the dice,
Vouchsafing me to throw them twice,
I'd opt for something more precise,
    I frequently have told her;
For I have come to realise
The Young Executive disguise
Insufficiently belies
    The fact of growing older.

But Old Executives, I've found,
Are rather thin upon the ground,
And why there are so few around
    Shakes my resolution;
For could it be that I am bound
To where a failed career is crowned
And ghostly Boardroom bugles sound —
    Last call for Execution?

THE SMALLER BUSINESSMAN ⎯⎯

I am the Smaller Businessman,
In turnover, not stature;
The future now belongs to me,
Or so says Mrs Thatcher.
We are a million or so,
Awaiting our deployment,
And if we each take on a man,
We'll beat the unemployment.

I am the Smaller Businessman,
But wish that I were bigger;
I'm told that Small is Beautiful,
But Big is on the trigger.
And what between the interest
And loans for which I hanker,
I wish my dear old Mum and Dad
Had trained me for a banker.

I am the Smaller Businessman,
Getting somewhat smaller;
And after tax and V.A.T.
My creditors grow taller.
I've found some customers to buy
On terms including credit,
And so my income only grows
Pro rata to my debit.

I am the Smaller Businessman,
Not taking on much labour;
Unless you count the wife and kids,
And recently the neighbour.
I've found the almost perfect way
Of conquering inflation;
For, since I can't afford to pay
They do it for the nation.

I am the Smaller Businessman,
Thinking of expansion;
And it seems the only way
Is mortgaging the mansion.
So, with my new collateral,
I'll back my innovation;
But not get very far upon
A terraced by the station.

I am the Smaller Businessman,
Depleted but defiant;
I don't suppose I'll ever be
Conglomerate or giant.
But something makes me want to keep
My little business flying;
And if I never make the grade
It's not for lack of trying.

THE ENTREPRENEURS ———————

The entrepreneur
Is increasingly rare,
But undoubtedly worthy of mention;
For the young of today
Understandably pray
For a regular job with a pension.

But a man with ideas
Now encounters a fierce
Irresistible pressure to scramble,
For a regular role
In some corporate hole
With a lesser temptation to gamble.

So the young and the bright
Who work on through the night
On the vision for which they may hanker,
Are unlikely to gain
Much reward for their pain
From the present day sort of a banker.

For the latter's inclined
To be more of a mind
To suspect innovations and think 'em
Less worthy to back
Than some dutiful hack
With a mortgage and regular income.

It's like slipping a disc
To be taking a risk,
If you don't care a jot or a tittle
For the maverick who,
With a favour or two,
Is a latter-day Ford or a Whittle.

And the money accrues
To the gentleman whose
Most consistent reaction is clear —
That an asset is such
As you count or you touch,
And you can't really touch an idea!

So the interest rate
Is enough to inflate
The rewards for the ones with the money;
And safely constrain
Any signs of a brain
With pretensions to dip in the honey.

But I don't have a doubt
That their talent will out,
Though the ludicrous system deters;
And I cannot conceive
That, in spite of it, we've
Heard the last of the entrepreneurs.

THE HEAD HUNTERS _____

The man with foreign sounding name
Was on my line again today;
For quite a time it's been the same,
But how I wish he'd go away!

When first he called from Biarritz
I felt a trifle flattered;
And breakfast meetings at the Ritz
Made me feel I mattered.

But that was quite a while before
I gained my board promotion;
Yet still he tells me how much more
I'd earn across the ocean.

And judging by the dossier
Possessed by this recruiter,
I sometimes wonder if he may
Be hooked to our computer.

So on and on, with knowing winks
He dissertates about me,
And half-suggests my Chairman thinks
He'd do quite well without me.

And how he'd like to meet my wife
And, over dinner, urge her
To taste the oriental life;
And what if there's a merger?

I popped into the Chairman's suite
To exorcise my fears,
Before the fellow's indiscreet
Enquiries reached his ears.

And that has proved, without a doubt,
The proper thing to do,
For now I know the gad-about
Has lunched the Chairman too!

It seems our universal friend
Is quite a head-collector;
He's also sending round the bend
Our Managing Director!

So now I feel no need to hide,
Or feel at all affronted,
Recalling with a certain pride
The day my head was hunted.

At least I would if I were free
Of lingering suspicion
That our man of mystery,
May be the opposition.

My colleagues theorise he may —
This mutual friend at large —
Be KGB or CIA
Of business espionage.

CULT OF LEADERSHIP ────

Since first from earth's primeval slough
Societies emerged somehow
And, retrogressing now and then,
Produced the dominance of Men,
It has been commonly agreed
There must be people who can lead.

The prince, the father or the priest
Met some criteria, at least,
For making in the infant state
Their leadership legitimate,
Though often, too, the biggest stick
Determined who might make the pick.

And then to leadership's chagrin
Democracy came creeping in,
With radical ideas which said
The followers should choose instead;
Or, at least, should have a voice
To influence their masters' choice.

Except, that is, strange to relate,
Within the corporate estate,
Where leaders, we are told, instead
Leap fully-clothed from Zeus's head
Protected, unlike other things,
By some divine right of the kings.

Suggestions that the lesser fry
Have any right to choose defy
The consecrated rights of bosses,
Whether making gains or losses,
To answer only for their sin
To priests who put the money in.

And those who hew the wood and hump it
Are firmly told that they can lump it —
A system known to learned sages
To mark the neolithic ages,
But now unknown to observation
Outside the business corporation.

So leadership, as a result,
Is consecrated as a cult,
Endowed with charismatic powers
Light-years from the likes of ours;
Particularly useful while
The new machismo is in style.

So might it not be best to say
That leaders, too, have feet of clay,
And any claim to lead is hollow
Unless the troops consent to follow?
If not, I think the special pleaders
Should find another word than 'leaders'!

THE DISTRIBUTORS ─────────

I pushed my trolley down the aisle,
Between the supermarket shelves,
And contemplated for a while
The eager shoppers help themselves —
As if in some hypnotic dream —
To frozen peas and clotted cream.

And, piling Pelion on Ossa,
Baskets bulging to the skies
With tangerines from Saragossa,
Deodorants and plastic pies,
They moved in ecstasy until
They reached the check-out and the bill.

Puzzled eyes, in consternation,
Watched the cash computers tick,
And struggled with the old equation
Of middle-man arithmetic —
How penny apples on the tree
Cost 30p. for you and me.

Observers of the business scene
Have clever answers to the riddle;
But to the customer they mean
The Law of the Extended Middle —
By which the price to them expands
The more the intervening hands.

The problem is they'd love to buy
The product free of all the padding —
The wrapping, brand-name and the guys
Who do the so-called value-adding;
And would so willingly dispense
With most of it to save the pence.

So maybe history was right
In placing at the very top
Of nations' economic blight
Their great obsession with the shop;
And, for every product sale,
An endless distribution tail.

So every item we produce
Sustains an office, shop or bank,
Squaring its hypotenuse
With costs and margins, rank on rank;
Turning my penny-worth of bacon
Into a pounds-worth of inflation.

But service-based economies,
The knowing and the wise insist,
Is where the richer future lies,
So maybe I should not resist;
I, too, will take the soft solution,
And keep my shares in distribution.

THE BANKERS

Oh to be in banking
Now that April's here!
And celebrate a spanking,
Profitable year!
Some prefer to hear a
Cuckoo on the wing,
But oh to be a Clearer
Now that it is Spring!

Better than the crocus
Peeping through the soil;
Richer than the hocus
Pocus with the oil;
Money is the medium
Surer than the rest,
For sweetening the tedium
With the interest!

Other men may hanker
For a bluer sky,
But oh to be a banker
Now the rates are high!
It's freezing, more's the pity,
The darling buds of May,
But down here in the City,
It's roses all the way!

Speak it not in Whitehall,
Tell it not in Gath,
Lest our little windfall
Cause Exchequer wrath!
Tell 'em it's for gearing,
A little more to lend
But mainly it's for cheering
Up the dividend!

Oh to be in lending,
Spreading joy around;
When every quid you're spending
Spawns another pound!
Loans are what we're here for,
Helping them invest,
Knowing they'll be back for more
To pay the interest!

Oh to be in Credit,
As the seasons turn,
With other people's debit,
Filling up the urn!
Never mind the weather,
Banking is the thing;
As long as we're together,
It's everlasting Spring!

PUBLIC PRIVATEERS ⎯⎯⎯⎯⎯⎯⎯

It seems that virtue has, of late,
Not seven deadly sins but eight
To vanquish and eliminate
    To drink of heaven's nectar;
The most pernicious on the list,
Our leaders currently insist,
Is one the moralists have missed —
    The evil public sector!

But none, more wickedly than this,
Brings virtue to the great abyss,
Or poisons with its vampire kiss,
    Our economic vitals;
And prompts the righteous and the wise
To exorcise the evil eyes,
By sacred cries of "privatise"
    To strengthen their requitals.

The new morality contains
Little to engage the brains,
But consistently sustains
    The ethic it's pursuing;
By which its druids blithely sell
The bits already doing well,
Which frees its acolytes to yell
    How bad the rest are doing.

Such fervent, self-fulfilling views —
Heads they win and tails we lose —
Are calculated to confuse
    The morally deficient;
Who, in their innocence, request
Why can't the public keep the best
And sell the market all the rest
    To make them more efficient?

But gods, the Delphic priesthood says,
Move always in mysterious ways,
And privatising that which pays
    Is in the holy verses;
While that which runneth at a loss
The Central Office omphalos
Decrees its devotees should toss
    To the public purses.

And so, to meet the Holy Writ,
We saw the branch on which we sit,
Or amputate the better bit
    With sacrificial axes;
Fulfilling, as the priest intones,
The message written in the stones —
That all the public ever owns
    Are burdens on the taxes!

UNIONISING THE MANAGERS ▬

Should we, since the times are hard,
Get ourselves a union card?
And, with all our Boardroom brothers,
Organise like all the others?
Should we bite the corporate apple,
And pay our dues to join the Chapple,
Or seize our Battleship Potemkins
By courtesy of Brother Jenkins?

Should we managers unite
For the universal fight,
And cast aside our corporate chains,
We Bears-Of-Very-Little-Brains?
Rise, and learn the magic jargon
Of rule-book and collective-bargain?
Show the red in our corpuscles,
And flex our managerial muscles?

Emulate, without concessions,
Better organised professions,
By which the other social gentry
Practise their restricted entry?
Be like medicine or the law,
Who closed the shop and locked the door
And, basking in their sweet communion,
Told us not to join the union?

Should shareholders and workers seem
Much better placed to live their dream
Than managers who do not bother
To be the one thing or the other?
Why separate, but fail to be,
The devil *or* the deep-blue sea,
Playing our ineffectual fiddle
Like helpless piggies-in-the-middle?

Don't we owe it to the kids
To sublimate our hidden ids,
And lift the lid from our repression
About the prospects of depression?
Would it prejudice our morals
To collectivise our quarrels
And mutualise our apprehensions
About the safety of our pensions?

But would we ever heed the shout,
"Managers, directors — out!"
When there seem to be so many
Substitutes at two-a-penny?
Maybe we should keep our chairs
And hope for half-a-dozen shares,
Or some discretionary bonus
From our charitable owners!

FRIENDS OF THE EARTH

We little thought that things would end
With OPEC seeming like a friend;
Or that we'd turn nostalgic eyes
To times when prices hit the skies,
And sing a eulogistic carol
For oil at forty bucks a barrel!

But then, at least, we stopped to think,
While teetering upon the brink,
That maybe there were ways to foil
The needless tyranny of oil;
And other methods worth the learning
To keep the wheels of commerce turning.

We even questioned was it worth
The raping of our Mother Earth
Or fighting never-ending duels
Like scavengers for fossil fuels,
And offering, in restitution,
A ravaged world and air-pollution.

And Nature seemed prepared to prise
The scales from our myopic eyes
And show what energies were there,
In wind and water, sea and air,
More rich, for those with eyes to see,
Than all the oils of Araby.

We thrilled to prospects of the union
Of man and nature in communion,
Harvesting the winds and tides
And energy the sun provides,
With some more promising equation
Between our needs and conservation.

While even those whose vision ends
With forecasts of their dividends,
Were galvanised by leaping prices
To seek alternative devices,
And place, upon a changing scene,
Their money where their mouths had been.

But economics, with their crazy
Politics of whoops-a-daisy,
Look as though they'll stand instead
Our expectations on their head;
And, with the price of oil declining,
Liquidate our silver-lining.

If energy renaissance needs
The impetus of others' greeds,
Let us, on our knees, implore
The privilege of paying more!
And may this masochistic pleasure
Teach us truly what to treasure!

THE UNDERSIDE OF ENTERPRISE

You know the game where eight or nine
People whisper down the line,
And "reinforcements to advance"
Is "twenty-four cents for the dance";
By the time the misbegotten
Message trickles to the bottom?
That's roughly how it grabs the guys
Underneath the enterprise.

And peering up the Tower of Babel,
From somewhere in the corporate navel,
Is apt to give the ones below
Communications vertigo;
As papers flutter down in legions
From pent-house to the nether regions
Producing, for the common herds,
A corporate flatulence of words.

And all this mangled up mularkey,
Cascading down the hierarchy,
Produces, quod est demonstrandum,
Asphyxia by memorandum;
Until what those on high intended
Is warped or otherwise distended,
With questions as to who's the wiser,
The doorman or the supervisor.

And as they multiply their sizes —
These Janus-headed enterprises —
And spawn division on division,
By dining on the opposition,
The aimless, disconnected sections,
Pursue their contrary directions,
Unable to resolve the riddle
Of what the head said to the middle.

So knowledge of the things that matter
Is roughly inverse to the data
Which shroud the monolithic giants,
Disguised as information science;
A state most frequently resulting
In fees for experts in consulting,
Grown fat upon the arcane arts
Of re-connecting corporate parts.

And as for the recurring myth
Of passing *up* the monolith
The views of these below the stairs
To those who breathe the upper-airs,
The evidence is in the scrawl
Of pained graffiti on the wall
Suggesting "Antony was here!
Could anybody lend an ear?"

CAREER CHOICE ────────────

Up at Cambridge, scraped a Two;
Stroked the boat and got my blue;
Wondered what on earth to do,
    With Greek and Latin verses;
Bummed about in Saragat,
Till father told me that was that,
I'd better be a diplomat
    And supplement the purses.

Sounded decent for a chap;
Commerce and related crap
Definitely off the map,
    According to the mater;
Pictured some idyllic scene,
Something out of Graham Greene,
In the service of the Queen,
    South of the Equator.

Met a fellow at the club,
Protegé of Pasha Glubb,
Mentioned Wadi-El-Khebub
    As a jolly station;
Phoned some Foreign Office guy;
Idiot suggested I
Had to be selected by
    Some examination.

Asked the johnny if he knew
Who-the-hell he's talking to;
Didn't know his Who-is-Who!
　　Gave him quite a roasting!
Said he didn't care a damn,
For who's progeny I am;
Got to sit for some exam
　　To get a foreign posting.

Finished up with little joy,
'Spite of being mummy's boy,
Disputing with the hoi polloi
　　The diplomatic cloister;
Conceding to some tyke from Crewe
The posting out in Malibou,
And having Inland Revenue
　　Suggested as my oyster!

Felt I'd had about enough!
Told the fellow where to stuff
All this bureaucratic guff
　　For choosing whom they're needing;
Thought I'd pull a bit of rank,
Joined a City Merchant Bank,
Where they're more inclined to thank
　　A chappie for his breeding!

THE COMMUTERS ⸻

Except for those, of sombre mien,
Who ride the lonely limousine,
Or float to meetings, through the crowds,
On chauffeur-driven silver clouds,
Executive morale is seen
Most clearly on the eight-fifteen,
Where business-men, in diverse suiting,
Perform their ritual commuting.

For here it is the sales director
Rubs shoulders with the tax inspector,
And factory managers converse
With broker, City gent or nurse,
Across the usual divide
Which job and office may provide;
And free from the absurd inflatus
Derived from salary or status.

Across the carriages they toss
The things they never told the boss —
Not secrets of the way they're dealing,
But what is is they're really feeling;
What more pretentiously is meant
By gauging business sentiment,
By experts too refined to crawl
Like flies upon the carriage wall.

And yet, some sense and understanding
Of who's contracting or expanding;
And who are bears, and who is bullish
Or where the order-books are fullish;
Who's laying off and who's recruiting,
And which collapses they are mooting;
All this is traded, fast and free,
Across the plastic cups of tea.

And much is written in the faces
Of those who take more silent places,
And sit, between suburban stations,
Withdrawn from all the conversations;
Or, somewhat furtively and solemn,
Peruse the situations column,
And, animated now and then,
Make markers with a poignant pen.

The business microcosmic view,
Is in the buffet-car from Crewe,
Or riding the commuter line
From Maidenhead and up the Tyne;
And he who swaps the limousine,
In favour of the eight-fifteen,
May find some unexpected gain
Among the sages of the train.

THE POWER OF POSITIVE BLINKING

Since wishes, as the young are taught,
Are really fathers to the thought;
And thinking, for the businessman,
Is for avoiding when we can;
And since our board had had enough
Of all this corporate-planning stuff,
Finding that it didn't suit us —
All this messing with computers;
We all unanimously stated
Thinking to be over-rated!
Henceforth we would value higher
The use of corporate desire,
And decimate the competition
By force of positive volition!

Scarcely had we made a mention
Of our corporate intention,
And the news leaked out as well
Of our boardroom wishing-well,
Than press and television news
Pestered us for interviews;
And the brokers ran amock
Marking up the company stock.

Academic commentators
Rushed to validate the status
Of Management by Wish-Kinetics
As superceding cybernetics,
Locating the astounding credo
In the corporate libido;
And, in a rash of books, rehearsed
Which one of them had said it first.
While every business school was billing
Programmes in Collective Willing,
Claiming Shinto and Islamic
Sources for the Wish-Dynamic.

Unions were quick to claim
Participation in the game,
Contented that the wages bill
Be settled by collective will;
And moved that plant negotiation
Be based on mass desideration.

And Government, whose every act is
Based on current business practice,
Lost but little time in hiring
The Head of Corporate Desiring,
From a well-known corporation,
To brief the Wish-Tank on inflation.

There is a move afoot, we hear,
To name us Business Of The Year.

ANNUAL GENERAL MEETING ──────

The Chairman's great phlegmatic calm
Spreads its reassuring balm,
Like oil upon our troubled waters,
Throughout the corporate headquarters;
And soothes away our worried frowns,
Across the business ups and downs,
With words of fatherly good cheer,
For fifty-one weeks of the year.

But, sometime in the fifty-second,
On past experience, we've reckoned,
Even he will fall, instead,
Victim to some inner dread;
And brood upon the now impending
Prospect of the fiscal ending
And his ritualistic beating
At the Annual General Meeting.

With negligible dividends,
The annual event portends
A day of unremitting terror,
And pained acknowledgement of error;
When pension-funds and institutions
Exact their yearly retributions,
And vitriolic widows brandish
Their share-certificates in anguish.

While some, with well-rehearsed finesse,
And eyes upon the watching press,
Will make pejorative assessments
Of recent overseas investments;
Or use their half-a-dozen shares
To catch the Chairman unawares,
Enough to give the Board the vapours
When they read tomorrow's papers.

And how the shareholders will treasure
Their annual sadistic pleasure,
Or revel in this King of sports —
Delaying corporate reports —
Until, the final insult parried,
The annual report is carried!
And, off to gin and tonics boasting,
Oh, what a lovely chairman's roasting!

While he, poor soul, his torment ended,
Or for another year suspended,
A double-brandy on the shelf,
Is visibly his former self!
And offers, to relieve the tension,
In words I wouldn't care to mention,
A few, well-chosen apothegms
On shareholders and A.G.M.s.

INVISIBLE EARNINGS ⎯⎯⎯⎯⎯⎯⎯

No human heart, they say, can yearn
For what the eye does not discern;
Except, that is, down in the City,
Where the Invisibles Committee
Is stirred to hidden depths of yearning
By what we cannot see we're earning.

And floating, as their name befits,
Unseen, above our deficits,
They conjure from the upper air,
Just like the man who wasn't there,
Mysterious surpluses of trade
From products which were never made.

So, when the visibles are slipping,
Or sterling dangerously dipping
Into its periodic voids,
They calmly levitate from Lloyds,
Or unseen royalties and fees,
The means to raise us from our knees.

Thus, month by month, they float the nation
By acts of prestidigitation,
Materialising from the skies,
Below the threshold of our eyes,
The cure for Treasury dejection
By extra-sensory perception.

I close my eyes to get a fleeting,
Dark illusion of them meeting
With vague, impressionistic spasms
Of men outside their ectoplasms —
A chairman, and his ghostly members
With poltergeistic non-agendas.

And, opaque as the general scene is,
They pull, like latter-day Houdinis,
Before our eyes see what they're at,
The earnings rabbit from the hat;
Then off! into the dark air gripping
Insurance premiums and shipping!

It seems the future of the nation
Is based on transubstantiation,
And economics of a kind
Where matter's subject to the mind;
The laws of metaphysics rule
In spite of what they teach at school!

They do say there be passing strange
Doings at the Stock Exchange,
Where, disembodied at the table,
They're non-corporeally able
To do extraordinary feats
With our invisible receipts!

73

THE JOB DESCRIPTION ⎯⎯⎯⎯

I trod, where fools alone may tread,
Who speak what's better left unsaid,
The day I asked the boss his view
On what I was supposed to do;
For, after two years in the task,
I thought it only right to ask,
In case I'd got it badly wrong
'Ad-hoc'ing as I went along.

He raised his desultory eyes
And made no effort to disguise
That, what had caused my sudden whim,
Had equally occurred to him;
And thus did we embark upon
Our classic corporate contretemps,
To separate the fact from fiction,
Bedevilling my job-description.

For first he asked me to construe
A list of things I really do;
While he — he promised — would prepare
A note of what he thought they were;
And, with the two, we'd take as well
The expert view from Personnel,
And thus eliminate the doubt
On what my job was all about.

But when the boss and I conflated
The tasks we'd separately stated,
The evidence became abundant
That one of us must be redundant;
For what I stated I was doing
He claimed himself to be pursuing,
While my role, on his definition,
Was way outside my recognition.

He called in Personnel to give
A somewhat more definitive
Reply, but they, by way of answer,
Produced some vague extravaganza,
Depicting, in a web of charts,
Descriptive and prescriptive parts
Of tasks, the boss and I agree,
Can't possibly refer to me.

So, hanging limply as I am,
In limbo on the diagram,
Suspended by a dotted line
From functions that I thought were mine,
I feel it's maybe for the best
I made my innocent request;
I hopefully await their view
On which job of the three to do!

ANYONE FOR TENNIS? ⎯⎯⎯⎯⎯

In the good old days we played,
Like decent chaps, the game of trade.
So, what the umpire said was that,
According to the rules of GATT,
Was taken, in the name of sport,
As ruling sanctions out of court;
And no ungentlemanly shout
Disputed when the ball was out.

But now, alas, the urge to win,
Has brought a breach of discipline;
With all the seeded players free
To desecrate the referee,
And go for game, and set, and match
By any rules their leaders hatch
Which give their overseas accounts
The better of the trading bounce.

For all the players it is vital
That no one else should win the title,
Though, what they can themselves produc
May get them, at the best, to deuce;
So beggaring my neighbour's trade
Is how the winning lobs are made,
While players, point-by-point, dispute
Who brought the game to disrepute.

Americans, for whom it's sin
To play the game unless they win,
Are most inclined to hedge their bet
By doubling up the height of net;
This stops the European ball
From entering their court at all;
While Europe threatens to retire,
Or raise its own a sanction higher.

But both accuse the Eastern set
Of dirty play around the net,
And call the Japanese a menace
Unworthy of the game of tennis;
Or fight about the repercussions
Of playing doubles with the Russians,
In case the Eastern Bloc attack its
Service game with Western rackets.

The players, to a man, deplore
The ones who call the game a war;
Insisting it is only played,
Within the spirit of free trade,
By gentlemen who don't resort
To cheating in the name of sport;
It's simply not the game for fools
Who keep insisting on the rules!

THE GHOST OF CHAIRMEN PAST

I loitered with a vacant smile
About the board-room gallery,
And contemplated for a while
Departed chairmen eyeing me —
A century of leaders, all
Impaled for ever on the wall.

Each beetled and majestic brow,
Sat brooding in its bed of oils,
And seemed anachronistic now
They'd shuffled off their mortal coils;
As if they'd nothing left to say
Of relevance to me today.

And mine, I knew, would be the face,
Within a year or two, no doubt,
To occupy the empty space,
When I no longer was about;
But could it really be that mine
Would be the last face in the line?

Whereat, to my eternal shame,
The founder, Thomas Binton, Bart.,
Leaned forward from his picture frame
And gave me quite a nasty start;
Suggesting if we sold to Carters
He'd have my rotten guts for garters!

And, animated up the room
The other faces, I re-call,
Attacked my prophesies of doom
With imprecations from the wall;
And then resumed their former places
Sedately in their normal spaces.

My board-room colleagues never did,
When next we all were congregated,
Know why we voted down the bid
I'd previously advocated;
But Thomas Binton, Bart., I think,
Gave me a reassuring wink.

And now I take my daily walk,
At lunch time, up the board-room floor,
And have a little private talk
With chairmen who have gone before;
I pray my own successor be
Insane enough to talk to me!

DEMENTIA PRAECOX _____

Since fear is all we have to fear,
    As F.D.R. was prone to say,
I launched my corporate career
    By casting all my fears away;
Speak up, speak out! and, most essential,
Display your management potential!

So, in my best dynamic style,
    I shot my cuffs and banged the door;
And, with assured aggressive style,
    Walked tall across the boss's floor.
"Shut up, get out! I'm in a meeting!"
Was all he said by way of greeting.

I set a later time to meet,
    Perhaps a modicum deflated;
And practised yoga in retreat,
    To get my psyche re-instated.
Breathe in, breathe out! — and off once mor
Ambitious, through the boss's door!

"So, with respect Sir, I've concluded"
   (Was this my former, timid self?)
"Your whole damned strategy's deluded —
   I move you put it on the shelf!
You're in, you're out! Your profit's shrinking!
You need some new, dynamic thinking!"

The silence which ensued was total,
   Though the thunder in his eyes,
Through the threatening bi-focals,
   Left but little to surmise.
Then up! and out! — his voice pursuing,
With "What the hell d'you think you're doing!"

So now I nurse my injured id,
   And feel a somewhat chastened fool,
Who tried to climb the pyramid
   My first day out of business school!
But work! and wait! — that's tough for me,
With 'A's in Corporate Strategy!

THE BUSINESS LITERATURE ⎯⎯

They used to say, or so I've heard,
In the Beginning was the Word;
But since the television freed
Our species from the need to read,
The scriptures are assumed to mean —
In the Beginning was the Screen!
For books are strictly for the birds
Since images replaced the words.

Which makes it all the more surprising
That sales of business books are rising;
Though Whitman, Keats and Tolstoy burn,
Executive desire to learn
Has boosted by immense amounts,
On corporate expense accounts,
The means to mitigate distress
For owners of the printing press.

And half our literature consists
Of vast, interminable lists
On "How To Ride the Product Cycle",
Or "Severing The Umbilical —
What Every Corporate Doctor Knows",
In crude, impenetrable prose;
Till every office-suite is lined
With insights on the Corporate Mind.

Executives who find success
Are now obliged to go to press
With autobiographic ham
Or how I got to where I am;
While business-school professors stand,
Self-effacingly to hand,
To turn the home-spun exegeses,
Into an endless flow of theses.

Since what the commentators write is
Prone to polysyllabitis —
The virus known to me and you
As 'why one word when three will do?' —
The miles of paper, pulp and ink
Consumed on business double-think
Have brought the publishers reprieve
And riches they could not conceive!

This literature, it should be said,
Is rarely written to be read;
But adds distinction to the walls
Of corporate marmoreal halls,
Suggesting, by its acquisition,
A touch of business erudition.
So few are destined to discover
What nonsense lies behind the cover.

CHRISTMAS PARTY —————

Welcome to the Christmas jolly!
Came round fast again, by golly!
Even though it's last year's holly,
    Here's to 1981!
Come on in, you girls and fellas,
Hand around the panatellas,
Get the vino from the cellars,
    Join the Board and have some fun!

Sorry that you missed your bonus,
Here's to all the City moaners!
Anyone prefer coronas?
    Fill 'em up and don't say when!
So, the situation's chronic,
And the customers moronic,
Pour yourself a gin and tonic,
    Consolidated floats again!

All these things are sent to try us,
Maybe someone else'll buy us
When the current loan expires,
    Bale us out again, you'll see!
Life's a bagful of surprises.
Could be that they'll nationalise us!
Here's to public enterprises
    Or, at worst, redundancy!

Cheer up, Charlie! Lord protect us!
Where's your faith in our directors?
Let's get out the new prospectus,
    Show a bit of business spunk!
Why not make that mausoleum
Of a factory a museum!
Can't you close your eyes and see 'em
    Flocking in to see the junk?

Give 'em all a bit of pleasure,
Now the money's all in leisure!
Part of our historic treasure —
    Why not call the National Trust?
Make an offer to the Nation!
Save a lot on automation,
That's the way to beat inflation,
    Keep ourselves from going bust!

Trust the brokers to ignore us!
Someone give us all a chorus,
Get old Parkinson to pour us
    All another glass of beer!
Everybody feeling better?
Told you we would never let a
Company Receiver get a
    Grip on all our Christmas cheer!

Right then! Lubricate your throttles,
Loosen up your epiglottals,
Lead us off with Ten Green Bottles,
    Another year should see us through!
Happy Christmas all you rowdies!
Down with pessimists and dowdies!
We could always call the Saudis!
    Here's to 1982!

BUSINESS MEMORANDA

When the Things from Outer-Spaces
Over-run the human races
And are sieving through the traces
Of the ruins which replace us;

Should they come across, at random,
Any business memorandum,
Do not fear! Nil desperandum!
They could never understand 'em.

For executival grammar
Would suggest a panorama
Where the writer tries to slam a
Piece of paper with a hammer!

Even Martians lack computers
So conceivably astute as
To decipher these polluters
Of our literary futures.

For the way the writer fidgets
With his syntax and his digits
Is enough to blow the widgets
Of the trans-galactic midgets.

Now their logical equation
Would assume that information
Is the prime preoccupation
Of this strange communication;

Whereas we who understand a
Businessman would never pander
To this vicious kind of slander
On his business memoranda.

THE BUSINESSMAN'S DIARY ⎯⎯

January: we explored,
At our meeting of the Board,
Why the year we'd just completed
Mustn't ever be repeated.

February: all agreed
Strategy is what we need,
To liquidate the Chairman's fear
On the current fiscal year.

March: unanimously moved
Action plan should be approved;
Especially in view of costs
Of three months we've already lost.

April: Finance Chief reviews
Prospects for our revenues;
Generally sad prognosis;
Sales Director under notice.

May: the Marketing Director
Senses he may now detect a
Movement in the market place,
If Production can keep pace.

June: the growth of finished stock
Suggests the forecasts all to cock.
Uproar as the meeting ended;
Half-year dividend suspended.

July: bank a little pressing;
Chairman ill and convalescing;
Plant on strike, but no one worries
Considering the inventories.

August: Marketing explain
New promotional campaign;
Quiet confidence prevails,
Possibly excluding Sales.

September: quarterly accounts
Suggest the wages cheque may bounce;
Chief Accountant wins reprieve —
Kept a little up his sleeve.

October: budget overspent;
Cut the price by ten per cent;
Advertising decimated;
Overheads re-allocated.

November: temporary pause;
Fire at main competitors.
Sales beyond all expectations,
Directors cancel resignations.

December: All the Board excited;
Rumours Chairman to be Knighted;
Letter to employees linking
Success with new strategic thinking.

THE CORPORATE MOTHER ⸺

Executives who meet together,
When the daily grind is through,
Rarely talk about the weather,
As other mortals seem to do;
Sex and business expectations
Dominate their conversations.

But, contrary to many critics,
This is not at all because
Businessmen feel aphroditic,
Wicked or promiscuous;
It's simply that their corporate lives
Reflect their mothers and their wives.

So, as with ancient navigators,
Dedicated to the sea,
Every artefact of status
In the corporate life's a "she";
Hence comments such as "down she goes!"
Describing Wall Street at the close.

So, that the dollar's feminine,
Or "markets" are a female gender,
Is not indicative of sin,
But surrogates for something tender;
And "matrix" structures are another
Subtle synonym for "mother".

American and European
Businessmen, albeit chaste,
Share a somewhat Oedipean,
Mother-oriented taste;
Their corporations, too, assume
Connotations of the womb.

For most executives of worth,
The deepest Freudian sensation
Is presence at a product's birth,
When all the traumas of gestation
Are sublimated in another
Offspring for the Corporate Mother.

DEATH BY MERGER _____

A corporate entity, which starts
As just an aggregate of parts,
Evolves in time, within its whole,
An idiosyncratic soul.

This personality defeats
Analysis by balance sheets,
The way your character eludes
The X-ray and the cathode tubes.

These tell us much about our health,
As balance sheets of corporate wealth;
But neither takes us very far
Towards clarifying what we *are*.

But what we *are*, on this strange earth,
Defines our value and our worth;
Not, for a man, his ears or throat,
Nor, for a company, its quote.

Yet analysts are prone to make
This odd but seminal mistake,
And think the rules of purchase hold
When companies are bought or sold.

But what the buying company gets,
So often, to its great regrets,
May be a useless bag of parts,
Like buying men without their hearts.

Financial analysts are, then,
The very worst of corporate men
To make so subtle a decision
As merger or as acquisition.

This may be why we see the trail
Of acquisitions, doomed to fail,
Abandoned to the Jack-the-Rippers
Of corporate life — the asset-strippers.

Above all, it's the people presence
Which permeates this corporate essence,
And catalyses, through the whole,
Its special chemistry and soul.

So synergies from mergers fail
Because the soul is not for sale;
Just as, when plants and factories close,
More dies than most of us suppose.

THE EXECUTIVE COMMANDMENTS

There are three things
That executives do,
Which the boss tells me
I must now eschew;
I must not speak before I'm told
Or interrupt, or be too bold,
If I ain't gonna grieve
My boss no more!

So I went on a course,
Interpersonal skills,
For executives who
Have obtrusive wills;
I learned how never to aver
And how politely to demur,
So I ain't gonna grieve
My boss no more!

There's another thing,
That I should not say;
I should not presume,
To a rise in pay!
For if I raise too much commotion
I may jeopardise promotion,
And I will grieve
My boss some more!

There's a special thing
That I must beware;
I must never ask
How the Board got there!
I must not draw the wrong conclusions,
Make pejorative allusions,
Or I will grieve
My boss some more!

The important thing,
In the corporate race
S' not to self-destruct
But to self-efface;
And he who does not get frustrated
Will be highly compensated,
And he'll grieve
His boss no more!

There's a final thing,
In this crazy song,
I must not suggest
That the boss is wrong!
For when my boss is underground
I'll be the only boss around,
And you ain't gonna grieve
This boss no more!

EVERY DOG HAS HIS DAY ⸻

When things are tough, I while away
The traumas of the working day
Rehearsing what I'm going to say
    The day I take my pension;
And after forty years, or so,
I recommend my parting show,
For, brother, what a way to go
    And letting off the tension!

The scene: my main director stands,
My gold watch in his clammy hands,
And jowls like india-rubber bands,
    To give his valediction;
And, to applause, I say I think
It's nice to meet the Missing-Link
When not, for once, the worse for drink
    Displaying his affliction!

And then to everyone's delight
I ask the chairman, on his right,
To step outside the door and fight
    And get his due come-uppance;
Or would he rather I announce
His special numbered bank accounts
In Zurich where his cash amounts
    To somewhat more than tuppence.

And then by way of coup-de-grâce,
I empty on the silly ass
The contents of my brimming glass,
    To shouts of acclamation;
And casually tell the fools
There's going to be a change of rules,
I've won a fortune on the pools
    And bought the corporation.

But just as I'm about to call
The Board to meet and sack them all,
The voice next door begins to bawl
    That something needs revising;
A hundred times a day, it seems,
He interrupts me with his screams;
What good's a boss who spoils your dreams?
    So much for fantasising!

ORIENT EXPRESS ⎯⎯⎯⎯⎯⎯

As producers of polythene plastic,
Our demand was a mite inelastic;
  For our business to miss
  The impending abyss,
Required something a little more drastic.

So we thought of a foreign adventure,
On the strength of our final debenture,
  To export expertise
  To the far Japanese
In a joint Euro-Nipponese venture.

Though their people were truly delightful,
Their devotion to duty was frightful;
  For the talks over-ran,
  In a room in Japan,
Two consecutive days and a nightful.

At the end of the talks we conceded,
They knew more about plastics than we did
  So we flew back again
  With a bank full of yen,
In return for our plant which they needed.

And we now, every Tom, Dick and Harry,
Are a Japanese subsidiary;
    But it's clear that the plan
    We reversed in Japan,
Has prevented our mass hari-kari.

And we've found our new owners so far so
Polite, with bows and their "ah-so",
    With the singular quirk
    That they're gluttons for work
When required to reveal that they are so.

Yet it does seem a little ironic,
The employees we thought so moronic,
    Seem to think that the Japs
    Are just bloody fine chaps,
And the rate of production's a tonic.

And the sight of our board exercising,
Was beyond any human devising;
    But our spirits and verve
    Grow in line with the curve
Of our profits and revenues rising!

TWENTY-ONE TODAY!

When I was one and twenty,
  And starting on my way;
And hopes were high, and plenty
  Of promise in the day;
The manager would tell us
  The future's with the young,
So come along, you fellers,
  And climb another rung!

To gain a reputation
  And mix-it with the rest,
With prospects of a station
  Up there among the best;
Work was a beginning,
  Facing to the sun,
With everything for winning
  When I was twenty-one!

Now, my one lament is
  That things are not to be,
For current ones-and-twenties,
  The way they were for me;
I wonder how I'd face it,
  To sense I didn't matter,
And be a crude statistic
  In the employment data.

Better, on the whole, is
   To have known a job and lose it!
But a youngster on the dole is
   More than madness if we choose it!
And will we be the nation,
   When historians look back,
Who betrayed a generation
   To the dole queue and the sack?

Beggars can't be choosers
   Is the counsel of despair,
The philosophy of losers
   Too insensitive to care;
Time the young were getting
   Their places in the sun,
From those who are forgetting
   When they were twenty-one!

(with respects to A.E. Housman)

EDDIE 'BONZO' MORIARTY _____

Everybody, hale and hearty,
Crowded to the office party
Eddie 'Bonzo' Moriarty
   Threw to celebrate the three
Reasons for his feeling better,
Notably his morning letter
Saying he was going to get a
   Rise, and be the new V.P.

Sadly, the elated Eddie
Wasn't walking very steady
When the President was ready
   To confer the accolade;
Quite forgot the boss's chronic
Hatred, verging on demonic
Of liquids such as gin and tonic
   Stronger than a lemonade.

Unabashed, with joy unbounded,
Eddie tipsily propounded
How his new success was founded
    On the cult of scotch and gin;
Singing from diminuendo
To a staggering crescendo
Ballads with the innuendo
    That abstention was a sin.

And thus did Eddie's prospects slip
Forever twixt the cup and lip,
Where others, too, have made the trip
    Which beckons all and sundry;
For he who dares to tempt the fates,
Until secure behind the gates,
Should learn the latin saw which states —
Sic transit gloria mundi!

CORPORATE GAMES _____

The Chairman will, from time to time,
Most properly exhort us
To cast our beady eyes upon
Events across the waters;
So the focus for the moment,
And the flavour of the day,
Are the corporate dynamics
Of the great U.S. of A.

In 1981 they saw
A series of ferocious,
Supercalafragalistic-
Expealodocious,
Totally fantastic
And unprecedented surges
Of the most colossal, corporate
Conglomerated mergers!

So the Number One economy's
Most fascinating facets,
Were less about production
Than the swapping round of assets;
And everyone gyrated
To the predatory patterns
Of the bid and counter-bidding
Over cocktails and manhattans.

The bankers and the brokers
Were the beneficiaries
Of this burgeoning bonanza;
And the legal luminaries
Were the laughing legatees
Of all the endless litigation
Which titillates the palate
Of the hungry corporation.

So they, at least, seemed happy
With their dinosaur-like clients,
As they locked their horns together
In their battle of the giants.
But other people might prefer
Their corporations thinner,
And cheque-book competition's
Not the way to pick the winner!

Just one or two are asking
What became of Anti-Trust?
But, federally speaking,
No one seems too very fussed;
And we all are now adherents
Of the self-same orthodoxy,
So will, no doubt, contract their
Merger-mania by proxy.

A Corporate Prayer _____

Bless us Lord, and help us live,
Like every good executive,
A life more selflessly inclined
To what is in our Owner's mind;
And may it be Thy wish, and his,
To tell us what his thinking is,
The way it was when we began,
Before we had the Corporate Plan.

Help Thy servants on the Board
Understand his words, O Lord,
Since he changed his erstwhile manners,
And joined the Long Range Corporate Planner
And if he needs must bore the pants off
All of us with Igor Ansoff,
Help us understand the charts —
Even the Synergetic parts.

Help us share his new perspectives,
That Strategies are not Objectives;
And, through Thy goodness, cross the ditch
To know more clearly which is which;
And, by Thy mercy which begat us,
Show us why it really matters,
In the name of Him who knows
All about Scenarios.

Grant us, Father, if you please,
Purer methodologies;
And tempt us not towards decisions
Without a further few revisions,
At interminable lengths,
Of our Weaknesses and Strengths.
Let need for action not deflect us
From codifying all our Vectors.

Grant, in answer to our prayers,
Thicker Strategies than theirs,
Who, in their blind unwisdom, chase
Profits in the market place,
Without a contemplative look
At what is in the Corporate Book.
Let their successes not distract us
From listing our External Factors.

Help us keep our Corporate eyes on
Some appropriate horizon,
Far from all the symptomatic
Signs of anything pragmatic;
Defend us, always, through our prayers,
From acting like entrepreneurs,
And from the uninformed who said
That, in the longer-term we're dead.

The author: Ralph Windle

graduated in Greats (Latin, Greek, Philosophy) at Oriel College, Oxford. He is an Englishman who, by virtue of an American wife and some years as a senior executive with two major U.S. multinational corporations, feels equally at home on both sides of the Atlantic. Currently he teaches business policy at the Oxford Centre for Management Studies and has teaching and research links into several U.S. institutions including the American Graduate School on International Management, where he is a Visiting Professor, Harvard and the Georgetown Center for Strategic and International Studies. He has held advisory roles to the National Economic Development Office in London, the E.E.C. Commission and many corporations. His published works include "Public Enterprise in the E.E.C." (Sitjoff and Noordhoff, 1978, joint editor and author; 7 volumes).

His Bertie Ramsbottom "Boardroom Ballads" appear weekly on the Management Page of the *Financial Times* of London where they have built a wide international following over the past year. They have also been featured in the *Havard Business Review* and many corporate and professional journals. He also finds himself giving animated readings of them at business conferences and around the campuses.

Bertie Ramifications Ltd.
125 Abingdon Rd.
Standlake, Oxford
OX8 7QN